This Is Me And All I See

A Simplistic, Realistic Book of Poetry

Christina Elisa Brown

Order this book online at www.trafford.com
or email orders@trafford.com

Most Trafford titles are also available at major online book retailers.

Note for Librarians: A cataloguing record for this book is available from Library and Archives Canada at www.collectionscanada.ca/amicus/index-e.html

Printed in Victoria, BC, Canada.

ISBN: 978-1-4251-2418-2 (sc)
ISBN: 978-1-4251-2419-9 (eb)

Our mission is to efficiently provide the world's finest, most comprehensive book publishing service, enabling every author to experience success. To find out how to publish your book, your way, and have it available worldwide, visit us online at www.trafford.com

Trafford rev. 1/12/09

 www.trafford.com

North America & international
toll-free: 1 888 232 4444 (USA & Canada)
phone: 250 383 6864 ♦ fax: 812 355 4082

"I have no dreams…
Only goals waiting to be accomplished"

Christina Elisa Brown

Acknowledgements

I have many and much to be thankful for. Without these people, I wouldn't be who I am today.

First, I am grateful for the Lord for giving me my talent and my vision for a better world. I thank God for giving me strength and joy.

Next, I want to thank my mother, Elisa Gonzalez, for giving me life and for working so hard to support my brothers and me. You and I are so different and yet we are the same, thank you for letting me follow my dreams and for believing in them.

My beautiful girl, Isabella, without you I wouldn't have graduated high school. Baby, I thank you, for being my reason to be a lady and to pursue my dreams. You forever will be my motivation and my inspiration to have a better life, because you deserve all that the world has to offer.

To my brothers, Thomas King III and Christopher (C.J.) Brown, there are no two men that I could love more. Thank you for being the strong men that you are. Thomas, thank you for being my father when there was none, we all try our best. You went above and beyond the call of duty. C.J., you are my best friend. You stood up for me when I could not do so myself, thank you. You are my rock. I always say that you are the only person who knows exactly who I am. For that, I am grateful.

I want to thank my dad, James E. Brown, for giving me life and for showing me how to start advocating and helping people in my community.

Belinda Smith, thank you for being such a good friend and for supporting my goals without any question.

Dana Clark, thank you for being there when I had no one and for giving me time and a place where I could heal. Your love and support has allowed me to get my life back together. I love you always.

To the Richardson family, thank you for your love and acceptance. I have never known what it feels to have a large family and I thank you for giving me that experience.

Mama Jackie, thank you for your words of wisdom and for being my constant reminder that the Lord is in me and everything around me.

I want to thank all my teachers and professors: Ms. Myatt, Mr. Robison, Mr. Connor, Mr. Grober, Professor V. Thomas, Mrs. Stephenson, and Mrs. Ehlers. All of you mean the world to me; I can't thank you enough for believing in me.

Ms. Myatt- I want to thank you for telling me like it is and for teaching me to expand my goals through education.

Mrs. Maureen Ehlers- I will never stop thanking you. You and the Hawk's Nest are such a blessing to me and many other teen moms.

Professor Thomas- You give great advice. I rely on your words to get me through my hard times. Thank you for being all that you are.

To my best friends: Jason Johnson and Bill Flowers… thank you for reminding me of who I am when there were times that I had forgotten.

To Leslie Overman, thank you for helping me and supporting me.

To everyone that helped me put this book together: Sam Park, Sai Sean Jones, Linda Haslett, Sharnaii Nikol Wiggins, Racheal Parilla and the staff at Trafford Publishing. Thank you for doing your best to help me with me dreams.

I want to give a BIG thank you to Branden "Chipmunk" Jones, for being the first to put your money where your mouth is, I haven't forgotten you. To the rest of my fans, which without your support, this book wouldn't even be, writing for all of you was the one greatest thing I could have done.

To my biggest fan… you know who you are, I'll never forget you, and you will always be in my heart. I thank you for making me realize that my writing is the key to my goals. Thank you for pushing me to pursue this.

To any and all unmentioned, thank you. Your love and support has been such a blessing.

This book is dedicated to

My girl,

Isabella Chasey Rhodes.

You make me want to reach for the stars.

You are my sunshine.

Preface

My daughter, Christina, started to show signs of being a writer at the very early age of six. I remember the day she wrote her first short story about a cat and a princess. As she grew up, school was her favorite world. Writing and reading was her passion, as well as her plans for a successful future. The way she expressed herself about her daily life experiences, my young "drama girl" continued to put her thoughts down on paper.

A young mother, she has always allowed herself to be creative and artistic. She teaches her young child to express herself by writing. Her daughter as well shows signs of being an artist.

Christina's poems are about the ups and downs of love, life, death, loss and all those feelings that we have inside. She puts them out there for us to identify or to express ourselves, within all those past experiences that we may have had in our own lives. Her poems are songs from the heart.

I have always been very proud of Christina. Even in those dark moments (and in her own ups and downs), she has always kept her dreams alive. She has finally accomplished her book. She has become my inspiration.

Elisa Gonzalez

Introduction

The reason why this book took 12 years to create is because sometimes I write, sometimes I don't. It's that simple. Writing is something I do for fun or when I feel I have something to say. I'm not one of those people who say "I am a writer, therefore I must write." No, I am one of those people who say "I write, therefore I am a writer." If it wasn't for all the people who saw my creative ability and requested that I write a poem, for them or about them, this book would not exist.

As a child I wrote fictional stories and planned for my future. It wasn't until I was twelve that I wrote my first poem, *"A Dream"*. A friend of mine motivated me to start writing poetry. We would share what we wrote via phone or mail. She lived two cities away and that was the only way we could "play" until I saw her on the weekends. The very first love poem I wrote was *"One"*. I wrote this when I thought of how two people came together when they made love. When I read that poem, to this day I see my innocence and my dreams of being *"in love"*. I am what we call a "hopeless romantic" and have been all my life.

It wasn't too long after that when I started writing poems full-time. I started writing about the people I knew and the people I wanted to know. I would write about them or for them and later give it to them, showing them what I thought of their behavior and their situations. I'll never forget when I wrote *"Love Can Be"*. It was about a single mom with lots of kids, still trying to find love in all the wrong places. I think I was about thirteen, it was the first of many times that I would see a grown woman cry over something I wrote. After that I used my poetry as my tool. A vice that would get my point across and help people to acknowledge that I could see, remember and feel like no other.

From then on, I wrote whatever I felt and about whatever I wanted. I didn't care what people thought but I also didn't ask. I just gave my work to them when I thought they needed to hear my opinion. It wasn't until I was a freshman in high school that I wrote, *"A Questioned Prayer"*. That is when I realized my work was a little bit more than okay. I was in my English class, bored, on the computer when I just started typing a prayer. What made me type such a sad poem, I don't know. But when I was done, I liked it. I printed it out and showed it to my two classmates, and I said "Look at what I just wrote." The girls read it and gave me this funny look, like my face was purple.

"Christina, you copied this out of a book." they both said. One girl said, "I think I read that poem somewhere." as if I was really lying. She was the one lying. I was pleased and shocked by such an accusation. I knew that they thought my poem was so good that it *could* have come out of a book. I explained to them that I just wrote it in class. Then I brought it to their attention that the only poetry in the classroom was written by William Shakespeare. They had to admit the truth. All they could say was "Well, it's really good." Even then, I did not see the talent in my work. I was so used to reading Edgar Allan Poe or William Shakespeare, and they had big vocabularies. Their poems were nothing compared to mine. Mine was so simple, so easy. But I continued to write nonetheless.

When I was 16 and my daughter was born, I wrote *"There Is No Me"*. She changed so much of my way of thinking and my life altogether. What had stayed the same though was that I was still into music and making business plans. I wanted to help teen parents after I saw what my peers and I went through having our children. My favorite thing to do was to listen to my friends make music. They would make beats with their mouths and flow rhymes off their tongues for hours on end. Rappin' or what we call flowin' or spittin' wasn't one my strengths though. I tried and they all laughed at me. "You're going too fast, slow down." they said.

Well, I didn't try that again for years to come. I did learn to appreciate the beat and to use it to create a flow within my writing style. So when they were spittin' lyrics, I was writing and forming poems. That is where I learned to love what I had to offer the world. It was my own form of self-expression. Instead of trying to be a rapper or lyricist, I took heed to the fact that I indeed was a poetess or what we now a call a spoken-word artist.

Right before graduating high school, I submitted my poem *"A Normal Teenager"* to an on-line poetry site contest. I literally invented it on my way to school with my daughter. I was proud of my poem. It showed the world that I was just as equal as any other working mother. Being a mother, young or old, holds the same maternal mentality. I was tired of being judged by people just because I was 17 years old with a child. I was still a mother and a student like the many others older than me. Well, I didn't win the contest. Instead they wrote back saying my poem was good enough to go in their book and I would receive a free copyright. That satisfied me. Just their acknowledgement as a writer was a great accomplishment. That alone made the contest unimportant because this was my first published poem.

When I started my first year of college, I was focused on getting a degree in teaching and business. I wanted to open a non-profit organization for teen parents and later I realized that the services they needed should be available to all teens. So that was my goal. I continued to write, for myself, as an outlet or as my form of expressions. Some of the poems I just made up while my friends and I listened to music. People still came to me with their stories of specific situations requesting love poems for their boyfriends or girlfriends. Some asked for broken-hearted poems for their break-ups or emotional poems when they were sad, angry or happy. I wrote them to the best of ability. Writing for others is harder than writing for myself because I have to come out of myself and be that person. I have to speak from their heart, not of my own. Thankfully it all worked out. I would give them a typed copy signed with my name at the bottom and I kept the original. To me, if they were happy with it, I was happy with it... indeed they were pleased.

Into my second year of college, it seemed like everyone knew I could write. I was getting requests left and right. The whole thing kept me motivated and inspired me to write even more. In the summer I tried another go at the poetry contest, this time by submitting about 6-7 poems. I knew one for sure would catch on. But they didn't. Instead I got the same ole' letter. "You didn't win but here's your free copyright. If you want to get a copy of the book that it's in, send us $50." I was disappointed like anyone would be. The free copyright didn't give me the same feeling of satisfaction as it did when I was 17. I was a student with a child and I couldn't afford to buy the book. My books for school were over $200 and I had financial aid helping me with that. Of course I wanted a copy of my work, especially done in a beautifully bound book. It seemed like I was never going to get one. Even still, I continued to write.

It was towards the end of the summer in the beginning of a new semester, when I had received a letter. Again, my poems were being published. This time it was "*Us Women*" and ***Love Can Be***". My friend was going over the poems and the letter when he said, "What would happen if you sent all your poems, one by one?" He surprised me because that question was so good. I had never thought about that myself. What if I did send them all of my poems individually? They had never turned one down.

I responded, "You know what? They would probably publish them all." I said that like someone had stolen something from me. I felt silly for not realizing that fact earlier. With that said, I started to rummage through all my notebooks, finding all the poems I had ever written. Pulling them all together, I read and chose the right ones to type out. Page by page, my excitement increased. I actually had a book of poems! Ones that I loved, ones that would forever make me cry, and the ones that made others cry. I also went over my notes from moments when I didn't know what to write, but I had to record something. I started turning incomplete phrases and notes, like "***9/11***", a day that we all will never forget.

I have so many moments and memories, belonging to myself and others that I just have to share. So many fans have enjoyed my work. They use me to help them express themselves to their friends, family and loved ones. They might just need to have something to inspire them or help them get through tough times. I feel like God has given me reasons to write and a purpose as to what my writings are for. These poems are meant to be shared, discussed and appreciated by anyone who needs them. It is my wish that my book helps inspire all those who want to write themselves. I hope you can learn that any writing from your heart is not that complicated, it's something to be proud of, not looked down upon. I pray that my work can be used for easing your pain or to give strength in moments when you feel weak. To be inspired to look at the world and the people around you as something beautiful and worth writing about is my ultimate goal. Like my title poem, "*This Is Me and All I See*" states…to any and all that find one piece, that touches you know, that I am pleased, cause I wrote this for you.

Lots of Love Always
Christina E. Brown

This Is Me And All I See

This is me

And all I see

This is you

And what you can do

This is my heart

Sweat, blood, and tears

These are my triumphs

My tribulations, hopes and fears

To any and all that find one piece

That touches you

Know

That I am pleased

Cause I made this for you

Of all that I see

And everything you taught me

The people in my life

The ones I've loved and disliked

Taught me how

I want to be in life

So enjoy what you read

Cause this is me

And all I see

One

Time stands still

The world is silent

No one is breathing

Moving or thinking

It's just you and I

I look in your eyes

You gaze into mine

Our doors open up

We reach each other's heart

Letting the love flow

Through our bodies

Transcending through our thoughts

Your soul swims in mine

And makes one

One life

One love

One thought

One goal

To be one

I Don't Believe In Love

I don't believe in love

Because my loves

Don't believe in me

I let them know

What my love can be

Still foolishly

They don't see

They blindly choose

That I'm like the ones they used

To fill a fantasy

But those females got nothing

Compared to me

So I say

Love is just a fallacy

True to those

That hasn't had the pain

That love gives

The sorrow that it spreads

And the promise

To never fall in love again

If You Want

I don't think you understand

The role you want to have

I don't seem to see

The life you have planned for me

Your actions contradict your words

Your lines seem straight

But I see curves

If you want me to give

What makes you happy

Then give to me some stability

If you want me to provide

Patience to your success

Then you should relieve

All that I stress

If you want to be

King to this Queen

On the throne

Then love to me

Is what you should show

If you want to be

Daddy or head of this family

Then you must supply

The security

If you cannot give

Then I shall not ask

But do not offer

What you don't have

If this is just a game

For you to play

Then no promises

Need to be made

It's easier than it seems

And still difficult

To achieve

If I give my love to you

Then give your love to me

There is No Me

All I need is you
To know that I am me
For without your life
Mine would have no meaning
In your eyes I see
What I need to be
Guiding you through
My mistakes and fears
Supporting you through
The clueless years
That is what I must do
In order to keep you
I'll provide
All that you need
For without you
There is no me

 A Dream

In my dream
The people are paper
I am the wind
Blow them away
And never see them again

Out of the Nightmare

The stars guided my day

And the sun lit my night

Darkness was blinding my laugh

To be alive in my death

I'm out of the nightmare

And into the sun

The raining has stopped

The love has won

No scenes of the battleground

No lamentation to be found

The war is over now

And the clouds are out

When We Argue

When we argue and disagree

My head pounds

Holding back my tears

My heart pounds

With rage and sorrow

My chest pounds

In extreme tiredness

Our voices loud

But our words weak

Us Women

Promises with no meaning
Like a man with no manhood
A child without learning
Such as a rose with no beauty
That which we hold dear
We are wasting
Yet we don't open our mouths
Sadly
Those who do
Are complaining
Not sacrificing
What they know will make right
Our voices
Weak, exhausting
From the complaining
That we
Were really just wasting
Our time
Of how a child can't learn
Cause we aren't fit for teaching
And a man won't be a man
Because sadly
Us women
Aren't fit for teaching

I'd Like To

I'd like to know
That you belonged to me
Cause all of you
I hold selfishly
I'd like to see
What you feel for me
So I can give
My love whole heartedly
I'd like to believe
That you would
Come to me
To be loved
To feel safe
To live free
I'd like to dream
Of my life with you
Without being hit
With life's reality
How can I know?

How can I see?

When all you do

Is held so secretly

Why should I believe?

Why should I dream?

When the reality of you

Is that you don't need me

Love Can Be

Love can be so unfair
Mother of seven
Stuck on welfare
Where's the father?
He don't care
I'm telling you
Love can be so unfair

Love can be so untrue
So many lies
They make you confused
Stay, go
Remain, or leave
What is a person to do?
Be very careful
Love can be so untrue

Love can hurt so bad
When you're brokenhearted
And too sad to be mad
You look for another lover
Hoping he'll make you glad
Listen clearly
Love can hurt so bad

Made a Mistake

I hope it's not over

That this madness

Will go sober

So all that's right

Can shine again

With you my lover

And my friend

I know I don't want this to end

Like two solids

Trying to blend

Denying to acknowledge

The others trend

To make it right

Where shall I begin?

For a stupid mistake

Such as this

Could easily be dismissed

Or you could say

It was a trick

I can't control or even predict

Your thoughts

And the ideas you come across

But I can truly say

That I would never

Try in any way

To make that smile go away

For in your eyes

I see brighter days

So don't go astray

Cause I know

I made a mistake

Mother

You've been there for me
Through the years
To make my days brighter
And ease all my fears
You helped me become
The woman I am
And on the way
You became my friend

Many moments
We have shared
From our dark fights
To times we cared
Still you are my mother
From the day I was born
To the time that I die
I hope that you are by my side

The job as a daughter
Is hard to be
But getting your love
Makes it easy
I hope this year is your best
And I wish you
A Merry Christmas

God Sent Me an Angel

God sent me an angel

At the time I needed him most

God gave me a love

That needed me

To hold him close

God blessed me

With the greatest man

He had ever made

Then told me

"Look in his eyes,

And don't be afraid"

So here I stand

To give God praise

For all his mysterious

And glorious ways

Cause God brought me

My angel today

The New

To me
You bring
The new
The new way I feel
When you look at me
So surreal
I feel
When you make
Tender love to me
The new thoughts
Of distrust
And insecurity
Makes my blood race
It's such a disgrace
The way each day
Now feels so new
Now because of you
The new way
Of hearing your thoughts
From the look in your eyes
I see the cost
All these feelings
So new
And so uncontrollable

My Boo

Guess what

Or guess who?

Can you guess?

Who's my boo?

Of course baby

It's you

Cause when I cry

I want my boo

And when I want love

I run to you

You and I

Are the only thing true

In my heart

We are never apart

Boo

You have no clue

Just how much

I really feel for you

Forever yours

Always true

Forever and always

You'll be my boo

My Angel

An angel kissed me
Then flew away
And on my heart
His kisses stay

I don't expect
Anyone to
Understand the angle
Cause he's my angel

God brought him to me
One day
Knowing he would love me
And the joy it gave
Everyone to see
Two people who were meant to be

Now I have an angel beside me
And when we're apart
My angel stays
Inside my heart

The Wrong Choice

What should I do?

When I'm in love with you

But you don't

Love me too?

It had to be

My blood

My sister

You want her

Not me

How could it be?

The true girl

You can't see

I'm a lover

She's a player

I'm forever

She'll stay till

Someone better

Comes along the way

You'd be yesterday

He'd be today

I'm Not Wrong

What have I done?

What did I say?

How do I make this problem go away?

I have no clue

About what to do

About this angry brew

I just threw in the stew

What was I thinkin'?

Without even blinkin'

I made a mistake

Sounded like a flake

And now I take

The problems that I create

And say that I'm the blame

I'm a woman

That's insane

So now I make things right

Cause the fight really wasn't

Too bad tonight

It could have ended

With more strife

But I know

In real life

What I said hurt inside

And now I can't deny

That I'm not wrong

But he was right

A "Missing" Feeling

There's no expression

No indefinite phrase

I have no real way to explain

This pain

When I think of you

To say that I'm blue

Would be an understatement

Every drop of this sadness

Cannot express my resentment

In everyday that I wake

Every moment I wait

For the dawn to break

Into the day my dreams

Go back to the reality

Of my life

When you were with me

To say that I miss you

Would be a mistake

The emptiness I feel

Is more than what "missing" can tell

I need you

Living without you is unthinkable

So with every thought in my mind

And every word that I say

I go back to the times

I got to hold you at night

Then my body starts aching

My heart gets to hurting

And I get this feeling

That I can't control

My emotions go

To a level

Or a state

Where my mind fixates

On the one man

Who kept

A smile on my face

I Say I Love You

I say I love you

No matter what

In the truest form

With the deepest of meaning

I love you completely

To the extent

That no matter what happens

I'm not leaving

You alone

To fight these battles

On your own

I say I love you

In my purest thought

With my highest beliefs

I love you completely

To the point

Of knowing

That no one can show me

A reason to disbelieve

What I feel

I say I love you

With all my strength

Inside my very being

I love you completely

To the degree

That no matter how hard it gets

I'll never give up

What some call fate

And others call luck

I say I love you

With complete sincerity

In this moment of honesty

I ask you to trust me

As I stand vulnerable

With this plea

Will you finally believe

That I love you completely?

Between a Dream and Reality

I'm so upset

I cannot breathe

I cannot conceive

The forces that be

These dreams that I see

And the reality of what is

Is a mix

Disguised in a trick

Or a treat

Seeming sweet

But full of bitterness

When it comes down to this

The reality

Now I see

But I can't deal

With the real

When I feel

My dream is still

A possibility

Such a fantasy

My thoughts of being happy

Are so funny

I even laugh at me

In denial

I be

About the reality of my dream

It's either too good to be true

Or too good for me

The Questioned Prayer

God, why do I cry?

Lord, why do tears run down my eyes?

Sweet Jesus who died upon the cross

Why do I bear so much loss?

I pray to you every night

And twice during day

Then wait for my problems to fly away

But God, why do my problems stay?

And as they go more come my way

Do you ever hear my cries

Of broken promises and unforgotten lies?

Why do you put me through so much pain?

Isn't your love for me what you claim?

Why do I cry myself to sleep?

Instead of telling me you are here for me to keep

I question you only because I have my doubts

I wonder what your love's about

I love you blind and endlessly

And pray your blood shed all over me

I thank you for my life and family

And ask you before my life is complete

To give me five minutes of happiness

Before you lay my body down to rest

But until then I wait for you

To whisper in my ear

That you love me and that you are still here

My questions will remain unanswered

As my life goes by faster

Yet faith in you is what I keep

And I still wait for the day we meet

For my painful years to end

And my life with you to begin

Truly you are my best friend

In Jesus name

I pray

Amen

Give Me

Give me your love
That is not much
But all that I trust

Give me your kiss
For nothing can
Be sweeter than this

Give me your laugh
For surely that
Is what I
Want to have

Give me your trust
For this can
Complete us

Give me your smile
So I can make it
Through my trials

Give me all that you bring
And don't worry
I'll take care of everything

Waiting for Love

Lost in thought
Full of distraught
An overwhelming aching
Of my heart slowly breaking

A kiss waiting
To be tasted
A love dying
To be appreciated

My heart beating
For your breathe
My body moving
To get you
Won't ever rest

Good Night My Love, Sleep Tight My Love

Good night my love

Don't cry my love

I am alone too

And when I dream

I dream of you

Just pray my love

Keep the faith my love

When everything is said

And done

We'll be together

And dream as one

Stay strong my love

Hold on my love

For all those dreams

That we have made

Will be the reality

For us one day

Sleep tight my love

It will be alright my love

When the nightmares
Are trying to creep
Think of my love
And you will dream
That's what I do
When I can't sleep

I think of you
So I can
Dream

Like A Normal Teenager

I am walking.

I am walking down the street.

I am walking down the street on my way to school.

I am walking down the street on my way to school with my backpack, books, and pens.

I am walking down the street on my way to school with my backpack, books, pens and a stroller with a baby inside.

I am walking down the street on my way to school with my backpack, books, pens and a stroller with my daughter inside.

I am walking down the street on my way to school with my backpack, books, pens and a stroller with Isabella inside.

I feel like a normal teenager.

Wait a minute that still doesn't sound right.

Isabella is walking with me on my way to school. I carry my backpack, books, pens and push her in the stroller.

I feel like a normal mother.

Choosing to Fit In

It's like I'm in the position
To choose myself
Or my mission
Or society's stupid provision
Of the ancient tradition
Of man and woman's place
Through evolution
And somehow
It came to
This conclusion:

We say we promote
Individuality
But we don't
When we keep
Similarities
As our top priority
In each little
Community
We reside in

The Problem

Your strength
Leaves my heart
Helpless to your intrusions

Your patience
Has caused a timeline
Of passion and pain and love

The length
Of our journey is long
And never-ending
But to start
Is to eventually finish

How shall we end this pain?
To begin the life we claimed
We started

This imposter
Of a relationship
You have to be
Friends to be lovers
And if we have covers

But no quivers
Then the shivers
Are more likely
Your cold shoulder

Against My Will

I want to do
More than what I can
Because as much as I want him
He is still my friend

It's best to wait
But my energy can't stay
Still
Against my will
I stay still
Not wanting
To face
Confronting
The problems
That lay ahead

I want him instead
This feeling
Dead
Next to him
I lie in bed

I need to control myself

For I could make a mess

If I decide to bless

Him with a piece

Of this

Need You with Me

Time has no meaning
When it's your love
I'm not receiving

Breathe is not worth breathing
If I couldn't imagine
You with me

Love has no wanting
If in my life
You are lacking

I Hate You

Everything about you I hate
And I think it's very sad
We use to share a love
And make each other glad
But your petty games turned old
And I saw your true face
I never want to see you again
So I avoid our special place
I hate you
I want to make my point clear
When it comes to loving you
I smell death in the air

Off the Top

Off the top of my head
I picture us in bed
Making the best love
I've ever had

Off the top of my lips
I feel your kiss
And all those feelings
I surely miss

Off the top of my breast
Next to my heart
I feel the sound
Of your breath
Wanting nothing
But to rest

Off the top of my belly
I remember you against my G
Telling me
How good it felt

Off the top of my thighs
I feel you slide inside
Leaving me
Nothing to hide

Off the top of my feet
I look at the journey
I had to face
And soon will meet

And off the top off my heart
I know
That we are not apart
And unto you
Is where my love goes
I know this
Off the top
Of my soul

You Can't See, I Am Here

In the darkness
With no light
To make it clear
You can't see,
But I am here

Out in the cold
With nothing to hold
You shed a tear
Cause you can't see,
That I am here

Trying to fight
To turn this wrong
Into right
Have no fear
You can't see,
But I am here

To feel alone
And want the pain to go
You think of home
And wish love were near
But it is
Though you can't see,
I am here

This Rage

It grows from my soul
And blossom in my heart
It creeps into my mind
Then splits my tongue apart

Words of hate and evil
That I never would repeat
Screams out of my unconscious mouth
From this rage inside of me

A softly whispered insult
Will tear my rage from within
But God can you help me?
And forgive me for my sins

Please take away the pain
That's buried in my past
Please take away the rage
So my love will last

This Game

I was wrong
To play along
With what you wanted
To be with you
I fronted
Acted like I was two people
In one
Trying to love
While having my fun
I never had a
Homeyloverfriend
Just friends
Then lovers
Then friends again
Never with it
All mixed in
Just love from
Beginning till end

So I don't know
This game we're playin'
I don't know how to act
Or what to say

When being with you
Is just talking
But I don't have you
To claim

It drives me insane
The rules to this game
I thought I could play
Without getting hurt
And causing no pain
But I was wrong
I was humming
The words
And not knowing
The song

My Mistake

I was dumb
To think my love
Would be enough

I was stupid
To think you would
Love me back

I was blind
To your disguise
Not wanting to see
In your eyes
You weren't serious
About me
Why must I love so freely?
To people who don't need me
I thought things would change
Once you saw how my love came

But I was wrong
It was my mistake

Love Is

Love is what makes you cry
Love is what makes you want to die
Or make you wish you were never born
Love is what we fight for
In times of need
Or in times of war
Love is what we die for
When we look in the eyes
Of our newborn
Love is what we strive for

When there is no way to find
Something that holds your sanity
Love can make you lose your mind

When you give
And don't receive
Love can be a hurtful thing
And sometimes make you
Not believe
That love is real
Or even make you doubt
That love is really
All about reality
When it really seems
Love is just a fallacy

My Love for You

My love for you is like no other
It cannot be told as friend or lover
It cannot be seen as happy or sad
But reflects the light
Of a life
Yet to be had

My love for you goes to no other
It cannot be changed or replaced
By some other brother
It was made for you
To hold on to
When you have no clue
Of who is really there for you

My love for you will never fade
It cannot be torn nor stained
Stolen or given away
The one true thing
That will always be
My love for you remains
And keeps me looking
Forward to another day

I Want You

I want you home
Cause I'm all alone
With no one to hold
And no heart to hear

I want you near
Without you I fear
That life won't be as clear
And I'll be running blindly

I want you beside me
Kissing me kindly
Loving me finally

Giving me what I need

I want you to be free
To just come home with me
To be alone with me
To be near me
To hear me
To guide me
Cause without you
I'm dying

My Past

My past is history

Full of fights

And lonely nights

Praying for time

To be on my side

Now I just ride

And let the drama slide

As time goes by

I can't help but cry

For all the times

I tried

To turn a wrong

Into a right

When I had no light

I maintained to struggle

Through the dark

On a constant hustle

To not pop my bubble

And I tried to stay out of trouble

Now my life is full of simplicity

Calm and chaotic

Yet obvious

To what is a mystery

All that I leave
To the powers that be
Cause He is here
And He will guide me

Missing You

I'm missing you
The way the stars miss the night

I'm missing you
The way old age misses its sight

The only thing
That makes things right
Is knowing
One day
You'll come home

Isolation

Today I'm in isolation
Isolated from what?
I wish I were isolated
Where no bad things could come in
Turmoil and pain
Stops at the atmosphere
The sun feels so good
It dries all tears
Isolated
Sounds wonderful
Isolated from people
Isolated from lies
Isolated from the children who cry
Never to see pain in their eyes
Isolated
Sounds like bliss

Too, Too Many

Too many fights

That end in resentment

Too many nights

I'm alone

Yet lying next to you

Too many chances

That led to the next disappointment

Too many romances

From a fantasy

To a long lost memory

Too many tears

I've shed

That you didn't wipe

Only a year

And I see our strife

Too many excuses

Of what should have never happened

Only one conclusion

That it had to end

Too much faith

I had in you

Too much trust

We had us two

Too many problems

We had to face

Too many tears

That you had to make

Too many times

I knew it was wrong

Too many times

I let it go on

Too, too many times

That's all I have to say

So don't ask why

It had to be this way

Too many times

I ended up sad

That's why too much

Of a good thing

Is really bad

This Love

To teach without speaking

To hold without reaching

To love without preaching

Is how in my life

You have brought new meaning

You took out all the deceiving

With intentions for pleasing

There is no mistaking

This love we're making

To want for the taking

A feeling worth embracing

Surely

There's no replacing

This love

We are creating

My Sexual Energy

My sexual energy

Is filling me

With ideas

That I have no business

To think

When I'm around you

I don't know

What to do

I can't even blink

When I stare and think

Of all the things

I want to do

My

This just ain't right

In my bed

But you're not mine

I mean

It's fine

But not what

I'd design

For you tonight

I want to turn off all the lights
And burn all my candles
So you can give me
More than I can handle

While I watch your body thrust
All its love and lust
Into one consistent touch
Till I've had enough
And I bust

Sometimes

Sometimes there aren't enough words

Sometimes there aren't enough pages

Sometimes the story never ends

But hey, that's what journals are for

Still today

All I can do

Is tell you
What's on my mind right now

And pray that it all comes out

Because you might not be here

Tomorrow

Because two
Became three
And three's a crowd
No need to pout

I just lost one
Or maybe two
Cause you wanting him
Makes me not want to
Talk to you

9/11

I'm scared
I'm terrified
To have seen all those
Innocent people die
I can't move
I can't leave
I can't blink
I can't do anything
I'm scared
There's people dying
While I watch
But what can I do?

First it was the towers
That blew
One and then two
Gone
With all those people
Who didn't belong
Or deserve to be hurt
And yet they lie dying
And here I am crying

Then it was the Pentagon

Oh my God

What's gone wrong?

Why? Why?

WHY?

Why do innocent people die?

Planes, but why?

Why when there are people inside?

Why when you give your own life

To destroy others who fly?

And kill all others that are by

To gain control

Over something you can't hold

Something that belongs to all of us

And without it we have no trust

Or can never be us

To take our freedom

Let it ring

Freedom

Let me sing

You say I know nothing

But I know one thing

I am free

And here the devil comes
Trying to destroy me
Those people who died
Those that we lost
Are my people even though
We've gone unseen and untouched
That might as well be me inside
For I never seen this coming
And I feel I can't hide
I know I can't deny
That apart of me has died

If it were me in Cali
I would need the support of my country
So I'll be strong
Believe my country
Cannot go wrong
If we fight for
What we know is right
To make sure we will
Never again lose
Our freedom like this

My Mama Done Raised Me Right

All I can do

Is keep my cool

Cause I ain't no fool

My mama done raised me right

Patience is a virtue

And there's nothing that

Can hurt you

If you keep the faith

In what makes life great

And to hold no fear

Except to the Lord

Who unto His heart

We are all on one accord

That we all want

The same love and mercy

Placed upon us

Yet we all travel

A different road

And we all carry

A different load

With one common goal

Yes, my mama done raised me right

I keep all my goals in sight

I know to pray and stay

Strong through strife

And in my heart

I have an ever-shining light

A lady is what I am

And a lady is what I'll be

Nothing else is expected of me

And what I know can never

Be taken from me

That what I start

I must complete

And when I love

To love unconditionally

Best believe

What you see

Cause my mama didn't raise no fool

She kept me in school

And when I was slipping

Through the cracks

Mama was there to

Give my ass

A reality check

About what I did

And what I'll get

You wonder why

I keep it real

Cause my mama done raised my right

If it weren't for her

I'd have no life

Or no courage to fight

The right

Or face the wrong

It's because of her

That I am so strong

And people wonder

Why we're so tight

I told you

My mama done raised my right

Denial

Stubborn and stuck

From the ruckus and muck

It's a disgust

Of the truth that hurts us

If you want

Add a cuss

To be blunt

It just ain't enough

Only the One above

Can heal your wounds

And give you love

No one listens to each other

There is no trust

Only arrogance

About what we've done

How can we break

The bonds that we make?

That we create?

Only to retake, steal

To hate and to kill

The truth will reveal

Those that conceal

The thought of knowing

The deal
Or the art of not showing
The real

Yet they still
Continue to not listen
With the mind cluttered
With personal ambitions
It seems like a tradition
Or an infamous superstition

And this vicious cycle goes
And nobody knows
How to stop it
And everyone continues to roll
In 360 degrees
With angles swimming up to their knees
And everyone seems to be displeased
Maybe because they too try to deceive
A friend that they treat like an enemy
That's why before my words get too hot
And set your mind on fire
To warm every thought
Let me tell you now
What I've come and brought
A whole new degree
But my angle stops

Tiny Crystals

Tiny crystals

From the soul

Rolled slowly

Down her cheek

With glossy eyes

And a saddened voice

I slowly watched her speak

"I know it's over now,

And I only have left hate.

But I don't know

What went wrong

Or if it was just fate.

I used to love him

With all my heart

Then suddenly

We ended apart.

I'm glad he's out

Of my life

And I bid him

Farewell

I realize love

Is nothing but a

Hocus-pocus spell"

I sat there

And listened

To the story of

Her flowered love

Of how the flower

Blossomed beauty

And rested by the dove

Yet when the flower

Reached its peak

The dove flew

And the petals slowly fell

With only dirt to meet

Even though she

Thinks he is the

One she hates

She must remember

This is something

She creates

And even though

She wish to never

See him again

She must remember

When she saw him

As a friend

Or a lover

That gave her a

Special glow

With the same eyes

That made tiny crystals

From the soul

Roll slowly

Down her cheek

You Forgot About Me

I cried all last night

Till sleep won the fight

I tossed and turned

Dreamin' of the lessons to learn

But found nothing to turn

This wrong into a right

I know you

Had a good time

Forgetting about me

While I cried for you last night

I thought you cared

When I dared

To take a chance

At this romance

Not knowing if it would last

But is saw something good

To be had

I wanted more than you

You want to have your cake

And eat it too

What was I to do?

So I just loved you

Gave you all that I could

But was misunderstood

And I didn't understand

How we could be

Together

And just claim

Friends

So the games I began

Trying not to hurt you

I got hurt in the end

Trying to prevent my pain

I played the love game

With no intentions

To mention your name

Or your presence

My actions irrelevant

Cause I had no use for them

Except to remind me

That you and I

Are just friends

But when the truth came out
All you did was shout
And push me out
To be all by myself
And so easily
You forgot about me

Hurt Again

I've done it again
Fell in love
Got hurt
And now
It's the end

Just like all the times before
I sit and cry
For love and more
To be with the one
That I fell in love with
The one that
I won't soon forget
But later
I will one day present
Some understanding
To this event

And I'll look at all those mistakes
As compliments
Of God's sweet grace
To help me learn
To prevent my mistakes

And to be stronger
With the grief I take

I don't know about falling
In love again
I know that the pain I bear now
Will one day be torn down
And all my beauty
Will shine from within

I just won't let it happen again
And if I get the funny feeling
I'll stop seeing you
Or even dealing
With someone like love
Because if you aren't making
The right type of heat
You'll get burned

For some reason
I keep mistaking
Or maybe
I'm just not seeing
Or being
Maybe I'm make believing
That love is even real

That's why I feel
That it's best
To give this love thing
A rest
Because I can't handle
Being hurt again

You Walked Away

How could you walk away from me?
When I needed you to stay with me
How could you yell at me?
When I needed you to tell me
Exactly
What to do
Cause I do all of this for you

It's hard to figure out
Someone you care about
You walked away
Knowing I wanted you close
You walked away
Knowing I need you most

Okay, okay
So I made a mistake
But it's wrong for you to
Punish me this way
Curiosity killed the cat
So if that is this
Is this that?
When you tell me to leave

When do you want me to come back?

Cause your heart

Is where my love is at

And today

My love

You walked away

Leaving me in dismay

Dismissing all the joy

In my day

Just like a king

Who's caught a thief

Or some boring commoner

With nothing good to bring

Or offer

It's just this one

That two

And then three

You're off with me

Whenever it's you

That's displeased

Basically when you walked away

You said off with my voice

And off with my face

I feel like such a disgrace

Since you said

Off with the day

How can I replace the little trust

You had in my faith?

Did I ruin everything some way?

Cause today

You walked away

Just Maybe
Love Was Real

Maybe I was wrong

To think this time love had won

To think love had just begun

Maybe I was just dumb

I know it sounds crazy

To think that just maybe

Love was real

And I feel

That those times were so surreal

I was probably dreaming

Or walking when I was sleeping

Because I was so close to what

Made me happy

And sadly

But truly

I wonder maybe

It was just a hallucination

A figment of my imagination

A thought from my creations

Maybe something out of desperation

All I know is there is a reason

Why God let me see him

Maybe so I could get my first love's closure

And my last love's exposure

Maybe so I come to

Understand

That love is something

I can't have

Just something to haunt me

In my sleep

Cause I was so close

To love that I couldn't breathe

And with every exhale

I wanted to yell

That God

Had brought

An angel to me

And most definitely

This angel did teach

Because I learned

That maybe I was wrong

Or crazy

To think that just maybe

Love was real

I Don't Know What To Say

I don't know what to say

But okay

If that's what is best

It should be this way

If that's what you want

I will obey

But when you ask me to speak

I don't know what to say

There's nothing left to explain

With or without me

You can maintain

But with me

You have me

No matter what you claim

Others will want to know

But there's nothing left to explain

It's hurting my brain

Thinking about how

To make this change

How to gain

A lesson

From all of your questions
But my body stays the same
Cause it's hurting my brain

I don't know what to say
There are no lines
For me to play
The music's come and gone
With your words today
I'm glad you
Had something to say

While I sit
Like a lil' girl
Who has been hit
By her daddy
When she tried to obey
Instead I'll take a hit
To take the pain away

To look at you
Brings too much pain
Your eyes
Disguise
Something
And your words

Show what needs

Confronting

But I sit in dismay

Paralyzed

I don't know what to say

To you

Can't Sleep,
Cause I Miss You

I never would have thought

That I could be so distraught

My thoughts

Would follow crazy actions

Only to recap one fraction

Of really thinking you were here

In one moment

The sound of your car

Had me walking

Through the yard

Laughing so hard

At myself

For knowing

You are not here

Oh dear

I think I miss you

What an unexpected tragedy

That has just come over me

To realize what missing you means

Of all things

It shows that I dare

To care

Of where

You be

Yet I think of you

Best beside me

Especially

When I sleep

For like tonight

It does not feel right

To sleep without you

By my side

Yet it does feel wrong

That you be gone so long

And me knowing

That tonight

You'll have no showing

Keeps my mind going

About what could be growing

Between us

Cause when I'm with you

I'm flowing

And without you
I'm gloating
Thinking about you

But tonight I don't doubt you
I can see why they loved you
Cause you keep it true
That's what you do
That's why I miss you

So what am I gonna do?
Try to go to sleep
Instead of waiting for you
To call
It's so obvious at 2 a.m.
That you're not coming at all

A Thankful Prayer

Lord,

I give thanks to thee

For once again

Saving me

I realize now

That this journey

I have faced

Is a gift of strength

And a test to my grace

Sweet Jesus,

I give thanks to thee

For kissing each tear

That shed on my darkest hours

For keeping me warm

Through the winter showers

My God,

I give thanks to thee

For loving me

In my times of despair

As I prayed

I knew you were there

I did not quite understand

Until I reached

The very end

What all the pain

All the tears

All that time

And what all those fears

Were really for

It was your wisdom

That opened the door

You showed my the world

And what it was like

For a little girl

You showed me

All the things

I need to fight

And in that lesson

I strive to make it right

Lord,

If you had not been there

Holding the knife

Then by my hands

I would have died

You kept me strong

To stay alive

I found you

And now the hole is gone

My gentle Father,

I give thanks to thee

You answered my prayers

You kept me safe

You kept me sane

And never did you leave my side

You gave me strength

And patience

Through all the pain

That came by

So I give thanks

Once again

To my Lord

My true

Best friend

In Jesus name I pray,

Amen

Addicted to His Essence

I feel like I'm flying
I'm close to the ground
Yet I'm higher than soaring
But just enough for exploring
What I never thought
Would actually be
I smile…
Cause this is me

I'm surprised how in the same life
I can now feel free
Cause he is with me
Right beside me
The man of my dreams
Whom I thought I might never see
Yes he came to me
Better than any knight
He came home
And made things right
He was more like an angel
And to this day
I cannot tell
Whether I'm still dreaming

About the reality
That not only
Is he in my life
But he chose me
To be his queen

All it takes is just one look
From my king
With the truest eyes
That I ever did see
In a moment that's complete and serene
I surrender to his love
In his eyes
I see the sky
And where my freedom lies
So with him I just
Fly, fly and fly

Closer to the dreams
That now appear as realities
To which it seems
That I might be in need
Of the loving that he's giving
Cause it does more than sweep me off my feet
It blows me back and sends me flying
And as long as I stay flying

I'm going to keep trying

To stay in his favor

Cause I like his flavor

And his presence

No man can contest it

Cause my man's got essence

And he's got me

Addicted

To his essence

Isabella

I know I may be
To young to see
Or know
The love between
A man and a woman
But from a young girl
To a teen mom
I transitioned
And learned love

Love
Between a
Mother and child
From wild to mild
And with the miracle
Of my beautiful girl
God started
Opening my eyes
To show me the world

Indeed - she
Was growing
And on October 28th

The angel's sang
A beautiful name
Isabella
My girl
My angel

Indeed – she
Is my angel
And she knows it so
I tell my girl
"You changed my soul"
She brought God to me
From within me
And since the very day
She came
I haven't stopped praying
Or believing in the Lord

Cause her innocence
Is as beautiful
As her face
Her grace
Is as elegant
As her mind
Which is smart
Gentle
Witty and kind

Isabella

You see

She

Carries this greatness

That leaves me

And all others in awe

As if we lived

In some fog

And had never seen the sun

She is the sun

She is our star

Affecting us

With her radiant glow

She's our angel

Pure of love

Suddenly You Appeared

In the middle of my life

In the moment of

My last breath

Suddenly

You appeared

Unable to take a step

In fear

You might disappear

I blinked again

And you were still here

No need to keep looking

My mission is complete

All my prayers

Were answered

For here you are

Before me

On an endless mind trip

On how

Timed slowly slipped

Into years

I thought you disappeared

Leaving no trace

Or clue

From what I knew

I would never see you

But God is full of mercy

And He ended this

Endless searching

For here you are

The thought of how

I've missed you

Wanted to kiss you

Tell you I loved you

Or just wanting

To hug you

Puts tears in my eyes

For here you are by my side

I'm so happy

It's unreal

I'm so happy

I can't feel

With you

Anything is possible
Together we're unstoppable
This shows
That God is merciful
For whatever my sins were
Forgiveness was given
When you walked in the door

Now I cry news tears
For suddenly
You appeared
Back in my life
Which now feels so new
And just like my tears
I live my life
For you

Mad at a Deadbeat Dad

A fucken deadbeat

Worse than the scum that creeps

In the sewers below the streets

The type of ugly

to make kids scream

The type of mean

That haunts your dreams

A fucken deadbeat

That's all I see

A child

In the body of a man

A man

Trying to be a child

And run wild

Yet asking for a chance

When you don't deserve a glance

Or a piece

Of my time

You're running around

Playing at night

While I struggle and hustle

And try to fight

For another day

For myself and my daughter

That we both made

Times have changed

And yet you stay the same

Years have past

Yet you still laugh

But this ain't no game

And I'm not jokin'

My temper

My patience

You've been provokin'

So I leave you

Where you be

To grow up

On your own

Without any love from me

Just because you don't see

My love doesn't come

From this bomb ass P

It comes from my soul

And the words that I speak

To lose me

Is an ill thing

For I am more

Than a lover

I am a friend

And once was yours

Before this began

And so

Just know

That one day

When there is

A man in your eyes

You will

Come to me

And apologize

A Sinner's Prayer

My Lord,

I ask for your mercy

To protect me

From all that hurts me

Please shed your blood

Over my soul

Just stay with me Lord

Don't go

This is the time

I need you close

This is the time

I need you most

Please forgive me

For all those days

I played with the devil

And went astray

I see now

Where I went wrong

Thinking without you

I could go on

When in realty

I need you with me
Cause without you
I cannot breathe
And with you
I can see
All the things
The devil brings
So Lord, please
Don't leave

Dwell in my heart
So you shine within
Show me the path
So I can begin
To follow you
Until the end

My God, please
Touch my soul
Take all this pain
And let it go

Forgive me, Merciful One
I am your child
And I cry for your love
This weight

Is a ton
And without your hands
My back will break
So save me, Lord
Before it's too late

I've made my mistakes
But you are all that is great
And through you
Anything is possible
So I believe it is plausible
For you to hold me
Once again

In Jesus name I pray,
Amen

The Way Things Are

If I could just go back

To when this first began

When we were friends

And we would talk

For hours on end

If I could just go back

To what was great

Before it became too late

Before we made our mistakes

If I could just go back

To what I did

I know one thing

I wouldn't do it again

Now you're gone

And without you

I'm all alone

I guess that's

The way it goes

I tried to make things right

Yet I was walking

In the dark

Looking for light

And in spite

Of my efforts

I couldn't stop the hurt

Or the stupid things I'd blurt

When I just wanted you

To love you

Be close to you

To show you

I could be good and true

To you

But it's over now

I can tell

With the way you yell

And the way I cry

With the way you don't care

About me breakin' up inside

And the way you hide

Whatever it is

You feel inside

It's obvious to see

When you don't kiss me

That I should just let it be
Because things won't ever be
The way they were
When the kiss was sweet

So now you leave
But before you do
Know that I love you

No matter what the results
I know I'm at fault
For the assault
Of my heart
And the reason
Why
We're apart

And no matter how you feel
I can deal
With whatever you choose
But you're a friend
I don't want to lose

Torn Apart

This feeling inside

Won't go away

In my mind I say go

Yet my heart makes me stay

Am I denying what I see?

Or is my mind

Playing tricks on me?

Why do you make me feel this way?

Am I just a game for you to play?

Is what we have a form of love or lust?

Cause this feeling

Tells me

There is someone

Between us

My attention goes

To what you say I should ignore

But what really happened

To your lovers before me?

I feel with you

They still be

Now in the same position as me

Why do you do this to me?

Is your love a test?

Or a way of torturing?

Another night at home

Alone

In my bed so cold

I think of how the story folds

Why doesn't he want

To be with me?

To get some of this

Sweet loving

That I've saved

For him

When will his love begin?

My love is there

To be cherished

And appreciated

Not just some spare

To run

Whenever he calls

If he ever called

I need one fact

One piece of proof

And when I find out
I'll send his ass
Through the roof
KABOOM
Blow his ass up

The way he took my heart
Except this time
He'll be
Torn apart

A Whole New State

A whole new state

A mental upgrade

A new time of focus

Now that the past

Is below this

Something atrocious

Now with the Light

I can show this

And see

Who could provoke this

Nobody and nothing

Else but Him

With that no need to begin

Or even try to explain

All the feelings that came

Through tribulations

And trials

All those hard pills to swallow

In a world so easy to follow

With a solid heart

And a body hollow

Everyday I pray

For tomorrow

For His forgiveness
To please be endless
And His mercy
To all that hurts me
Strength He has given
For I have seen
All that I have risen
Indeed a gift
Was His wisdom
For without it
I'd be in prison

Now after all that I've been in
I can see a whole new life about to begin
Where I can be free
To just be me
And all that I can be
With my objectives
Now clear and visible to see
And even though
Not every goal is complete
Like dominoes
Each obstacle
Will see defeat
Cause He is my retreat
To all that sorrows me

Life can be so amazing

And still so bittersweet

My mind is going crazy

And my body is about to breakdown

Put do I frown?

No

Of course not

Then all others will be distraught

About all their problems

That I forgot

To remember

While my battles

I fought

Alone

Yeah I called

But no one was home

Yet if you need something

Guess who's on the phone?

I feel like a drone

I bore only one child

Yet I have many to raise

What is this, a faze?

Feels more like a maze

With me trying to find my way

Hey I know I'm young in age

But there is more to this book

Then just one page

And my memory doesn't fade

That's why the jack of all trades

Still refers to me as the spade

So now I wait

for the day

That I break

Cause everyday

I try to make

The best of things

But the devil always brings

Something

To destroy me

Maybe God is whispering

And life is too loud for listening

So I just calm down

And look around

At all the many things

And the many gifts I've received

Then I hear His words

And I'm thankful indeed

The Others Before Me

I am who I am

Because of the others before me

I know now that they

Did not ignore me

But really adored me

Now I see throughout history

What the struggles about

And now

What I must be

I tell you- I am

WHO I am

Because of the others before me

They showed me that one day

We can have the glory

Or at least help to decrease

The prejudices

Which increases the peace

And I know we ALL

Got some stories

I know, now

That I am

Who I am

Because of the others before me

I also know that many of you

Have seen the glory

Whether in a dream

Or just a thought

Maybe, even, as a reality

Of a possibility

If we all stopped complaining

About the things we could be changing

If we all could just stop

Being so lazy

The things we could do amazes me

So I say I am

Who I am

Because of the others

Before me

Tell me

Are you listening?

Are you envisioning?

What you can do

To affect OUR history

Or what will be history

If we do what we foresee

Then maybe

The mission could be complete

We've read

How the hatred was bred

And we've seen the beatings

The mistreatings

And the abuse of authority

What I see amongst the youth

Now is boring me

They act like they're two

When the age range is twenty

And if I speak of you

Please don't be offended

But if you've seen

What I've seen

Then you would agree

The complaints-

Plenty

The violence-

Mass killings

The tears-

Overflowing

All these efforts made

Are going the wrong way

On a destructive path

With that what future

Will we have?
What future will we give
If we don't live our lives today
Focused on a better tomorrow?

I Can't Take It You Two

Part Two

I can't take it
Or shake it
This feeling
Can't make it

Before I go crazy
Looking at how
You so easily
Betrayed me

Selfish I think
I can be
But this time
It's only
Selfish I see

We were suppose
To be so deep
Now I see
It's easy

For shit to get

In between

It's like you reached

For my heart

And took out my spleen

Looking at you

Makes my eyes

Start burning

While I'm gasping for air

I say a prayer

That this feeling

Will go away

I get so weak in the knees

I have to sit

But I won't quit

Walking away

From you

Far away

From the view

Of you

Doing what you do

As if I weren't here

But I am here
And even worse
I would have been
In your shoes
If I hadn't
Given him access
To you
What a stupid thing to do

And to remind me
Of my stupidity
You sit and laugh at my feelings
By continuing to do
What you do

Now I have no clue
Nor an idea
On how I'm getting
Outta her
Cause I can't deal
With this thing
That I feel

And there's no way

I'll be the bad guy today

By saying anything

That might bring

Unhappiness

To someone

I call my friend

But there is no trust in this

Cause you still do this

As if I don't care

When I tell you

My dreams became nightmares

When you two

Are there

Acting the way you do

Like today

Did I misplace

Or mistake

Our friendship some way?

As if saying something

Really would have

Mattered anyway

And for you to

Throw it in my face

By giving me no place

To get some space

To just get away

From this disgrace

Of what was suppose

To be friendship

How close

Were we

For you to choose

Him over me?

That's why

I can't take it

About to cry

But trying to fake

That everything's cool

So now I have a headache

Only A Season

This is only a season
I have to keep believin'
That this...
Is only a season

I'm out here
All alone
And even when
I find a home
My rooms will lie empty
Just as I feel now
Just the same
I'm empty
Without my child

A wandering soul
Amongst the madness
The sadness
From the lack
Of my one distraction
My seed

Amongst whom

I watched a flower bloom
From a beautiful baby
To an extraordinary little lady
And like the seasons
Of her infanthood
My love for her is understood
In many fazes and stages
Yet all stay amongst
The pages of the same book

Motherhood
Is the life I took
And even more so
Chose to live
And with that I give
All my love to her

Which goes beyond
All seasons
At the very epitome
My love for her
Is beyond infinity
And it's killing me

To not have her
Here

To hold
To mold
Or to laugh and play with
Sometimes I feel
I can't make it

This negativity
I know
I have to shake it
Cause the relativity
Is that my child is
A reflection
Of the life that I give
To her
On a daily basis

So these challenges
I'll face them
Indefinitely
I can't leave
My baby
Alone

When we talk on the phone
She tells me she's okay
But the other day

When she sang
A new song
That she made
From her brain

It came
To be
The saddest song
About how things went wrong
And now
She has no clue
On what to do
About being alone

With me
Her own mama
On the phone

Oh it is a sad day
To hear your baby say
She is alone
Because only the love
That I give
Makes her feel
At home

And from the tone

In her voice

She is not okay

So what did I say

In response to her song?

That it was beautiful

And to just hold on

It won't be long

For all hard days

Will soon be gone

And to just keep praying

Cause her and I can make it

With God's help and patience

And when the phone clicked

Cause we said our good-byes

I just sat

And cried

And cried

And said

"God

I know you're right

But I don't see why

I have to go through this strife

So I just pray

To give thanks
And to ask you to stay
Beside me"

"It's my daughter
You see
I feel like I can't keep going
But I'm knowing
That she needs her mommy
And I'm tired of calling
When she should be living
With me
So I plea
Forgive me
For my treason"

And God whispered
"This is only a season"

The Role and the Need
Of a King
In the Eyes
Of His Queen

Your position

As my chosen King

Is now more

Than a blessing

It is your calling

For you have now become

The only one

To know

Who I am

And the only one

To know

Where I want to be

Unfailingly

And forever willingly

You made sure

That I could see

That I could understand

The different situations

At hand

And most importantly
What a real
Relationship means
You made it clear
How we could build
A solid foundation
Together
Using our faith
In God
And each other

The stress these days
Is our greatest challenge
Yet we have managed
To keep our love
In it's form
Where it stays strong
And still
We long
To be together

The efforts we made
To be honest
To communicate
And to trust
Are phenomenal

For a couple like us

No one can deny

That we both continue

To not give up

Regardless of the obstacles

Or the challenges

The mistakes we faced

The tears

The debates

Are all stepping stones

To the higher place

That we've displayed

As our destination

Our place to play

Where the King and Queen

Are both at reign

And lay upon their throne

We both know

What we have is great

And no one can touch

Or even glimpse

The extensions

To the comprehensions

Of our greatness

That is why

I can't let you go

You have shown me

Who I am

Who I want to be

And who I am meant to be

Your Queen

Like a King

You humbled me

Proving His existence

With your presence

Intensifying my faith

I got addicted

Already knowing

I am in love

Your love

In return

Is a blessing

With force

And humility

You educated me

About love and life

Showing the pain

In the efforts

And the gain

From the sacrifice

You kept me on

The same page as you

You brought my mind

To a place where

I had not yet reached

Your knowledge

Gives my potential

Power

Unlike any other

Relationship

You uplifted my spirit

With your showmanship

Your advice

Safeguards

My thoughts

And protects my heart

Your words stay with me

Constantly

Affecting my movements

Down to my very being

You've changed me

By leading me

Guiding me

Into a stronger woman

Making me

A better friend

To myself

And my family

Now my voice has more strength

My words more depth

My life more focus

And because of this

I am blessed

That is why

I still pray

That one day

I can be

A great wife

For you

My King

And I accept

That responsibility

I know what I want now

And I know your expectations

As well as the consequences

Of my actions

I am no longer afraid

Or uncertain

Of myself

Or of what I am called to do

You have proven to me

This love is worth it

Your love is great

Your support

Gives me confidence

And the motivation

To do my best

And to not give in

To defeat

Or the temptations

Of the flesh

You're my highest believer

My truest fan

Without you

I wouldn't have seen

The woman

That I am

Or who I was suppose to be

You were the one

Who believed

In me the most

You keep me going

Everyday

Knowing

That everyday

I will make progress

And I now take pleasure

Knowing that you will

Soon see the success

Now

How I rest

How I stand

Is a reflection of you

And who I am

What you've taught me

Is apart

Of my being

In my heart

Your faith

Gives me an abundance

Of strength

Your love for me

Overwhelms me with joy

And fills me with pride

Now I feel

I can do anything

With no fear

No doubt

Just faith

And trust

In what God has given me

Us

With that I ask

For you to understand

Why I feel so strongly

About your calling

And my reasons

For believing

That you were made for me

That I was made for you

It was the Lord who knew

That I needed you

This is why I plead

No matter what happens

To you my King

Do not make me leave

No matter what is at stake

Ask me to stay

Ask me to pray

Ask me to do anything

But go away

Life without you

I don't want to face

No matter where

No matter when

No matter how

Time and space

Takes our life

I want to be the one

You take

As your wife

Vows of Faith
From the Queen

My position

As your chosen Queen

Is now more

Than a calling

It is my blessing

For I am now

Beside a great King

And you are

The man of my dreams

So in this reality

I refuse

To let anything

Keep me

From you

Time and space

Just creates

Obstacles

Challenges

Nothing that life

Doesn't already promise

Like life

These vows

Are made

Because like life

I cannot escape

The beauty

In the gifts

That God creates

So I keep my faith

In Him

And with that said

I use this pen

To express

What the Lord

Has called for me to do

To lay my vows

Of faith

To Him

And to you

I will say yes

To any and all

That you request

I will sit at your feet

And place my head in your lap

For comfort and safekeeping

I will place my heart in your hands

Giving you my strength

And my weakness

I will give no thought

Or no chance

To the opportunities

That can destroy us

I will honor your presence

By living

Accordingly

And obeying your guidance

I will hold no uncertainty

To what you tell me

I will no longer doubt

You

Or be afraid

Of the conclusions

Leaving the door open

To all kinds

Of confusions

And delusions

Instead I will take heed

And believe

You

And all that you present

Knowing with full confidence

That your heart is pure

And more than capable

Of respecting and loving

Me

Which you do

So satisfyingly

You

Make me a priority

Striving to keep

Me not just happy

But fulfilled

This is my vow

As your Queen

To have faith

In you

My King

To hold faith

As my highest priority

And to keep the faith

In God

Who answers all those

Who keep

The faith

In Him